W9-ABW-261

For Léa,

Thanks to Marie-Dominique de Teneuille,
Béatrice Foulon, Frédérique Kartouby,
Hugues Charreyron and Annick Duboscq.

In the same collection
My little Cluny
My little Louvre
My little Picasso
My little Orangerie
My little Quai Branly
My little Versailles
My little Pompidou Centre
My little Guimet
My Luxembourg

Translation Isabel Ollivier
Design and layout Chloé Bureau du Colombier
Photoengraving Haudressy
Printed by Imprimerie Gibert Clarey, Chambray-lès-Tours, France

Cover illustration:
a detail from *The Ball* by Félix Vallotton

Marie Sellier

My Little Orsay

m

The Orsay Museum has two big round eyes that watch the Seine flow by.

Are they eyes? No, they are clocks!

Two big round clocks.

What are the clocks for? Silly billy!

So we won't miss the train, of course.

Because, before it was a museum, Orsay was a railway station,

full of engines and luggage and passengers.

Now the trains have gone.

There are paintings, statues and beautiful things, instead.

And...

there is... a red dog

Yes, I'm red. What of it?

Nobody owns me,

I'm a stray dog.

I live a dog's life,

just as I please.

But I like the pretty vahine

playing Tahitian tunes

on her little flute,

because sometimes

she gives me

a bowl of soup to lap.

Paul Gauguin
Arearea
1892

Vincent's room is yellow and blue.

Everything is neat and tidy:

his washing things are on the table,

the chair is beside the bed,

the clothes are on the peg,

the bed has been made.

Vincent is an artist.

He did the paintings on the wall.

He even painted himself.

You can see his face

over the bed,

on the left.

Vincent van Gogh
Van Gogh's Bedroom at Arles
1889

there is... a little prince and his dog

My name's Eugene. I'm nine.

My dad's the Emperor.

It's a bit boring in the palace sometimes

because I have no brothers and sisters.

But I'm lucky to have Nero.

He's my dog. Mr Carpeaux,

who is a great sculptor,

carved Nero and me out of

a big block of white marble.

We got pins and needles in our feet

from standing still for so long!

Jean-Baptiste Carpeaux
The Crown Prince and his Dog
1865

there is... a big garden

"Granny, please,

may I have some more orangeade?"

Charles is asking.

Granny never says no

to her grandchildren.

She is delighted to have them

around her during the holidays.

It is a lovely, lazy summer afternoon!

Dad is having a nap,

Mum is playing with the white kitten,

our dog, Blacky, is dozing in the sun

and Uncle Peter is painting us all.

Pierre Bonnard
Middle-Class Afternoon
1900

15

there are... dancing girls in blue tutus

In the Opera House,

there are ballerinas

in fluffy tutus and pink slippers,

who dance on the tips of their toes.

Mr Edgar was enchanted.

He collected them

like butterflies

and popped them

in his sketchbook.

Edgar
Degas
The
Blue
Dancers
about
1893

there are ... three people on a balcony

One, two, three,

a fan, a blond moustache and a pair of silk gloves.

One man and two ladies,

a blue tie, white dresses and an umbrella,

between two green shutters

on the big iron balcony.

They are not talking,

they are not even looking

at each other.

So what are they doing there,

together but separate,

on the big iron balcony?

Édouard Manet
The Balcony
1868-1869

there are ... oranges and apples
rolling on a white cloth

Where are the apples?

Where are the oranges?

It's hard to say

because the apples

are sometimes orange,

and the oranges

often look like apples.

They make a funny fruit salad,

all those apples and oranges

playing hide-and-seek

on the humpy-bumpy tablecloth.

They nearly make you dizzy!

Paul Cézanne
Apples and Oranges
1895-1900

21

there are ... people on chairs, looking at the sea

When Mr Boudin goes to the beach,

he takes his paint box with him.

He paints ladies

and gentlemen chatting,

children wriggling,

dogs trotting

along the sand.

He paints them all tiny

under the wide skies

of Normandy.

Eugène Boudin
Trouville Beach
1869

there is... a big lion

I am the King of the Beasts.

I am so big and strong

that they put my statue

in the museum.

I sit perfectly still.

No clawing

or roaring.

I'm there to be admired.

Aren't I the handsomest beast of all?

Antoine-Louis Barye
Great Seated Lion
1887

there is... a magpie out in the cold

Magpie, magpie,

what are you doing there,

all alone on the fence?

You're such a chatterbox

and there's no one to talk to!

It is too cold.

Freezing cold.

There is not a soul outside.

But you're right to be out and about.

How pretty the countryside is,

all grey-blue shadows

on bright white snow.

Claude Monet
The Magpie
1868-1869

27

there is... a big smooth polar bear

I am a polar bear, smooth all over

in my big white fur coat.

Not a fold or a hair

out of place.

I'm glad to be

so cosy in the cold.

The man who made me

so smooth

has a funny round name.

He is called Pompon.

Pompon
Polar Bear
1918-1929

29

there is... a lady on a swing

"Will Mummy give me a turn
on the swing soon?" wonders Jane.
But Jane's mummy is dreaming.
She is dreaming as she watches
the patches of sunlight rolling
over the ground like gold coins.
She is dreaming
that a will-o'-the-wisp
danced by, murmuring:
"You are as pretty as a picture
in your blue and white frock!"
But was it really a dream?

Pierre-Auguste
Renoir
The Swing
1876

there is... a child chasing a red ball

What can the magpie see from the top of the tree?

A yellow straw hat and a red ball.

A lady in blue and a lady in white.

But...

is the child in the yellow straw hat

a little girl? Or a boy

with long hair?

And...

Who is

the child's mother?

The lady in blue,

or the lady in white?

The magpie cannot tell!

Félix Vallotton
The Ball
1899

there is... a little baby fast asleep

Shh! He's sleeping...
Gently, very gently,
Mummy lifts aside
the white netting.
And softly, very softly, she sings:
"Sleep, my butterfly, my little dragonfly,
sleep my golden child, mummy's here..."

Berthe Morisot
The Cradle
about 1872

there is... a circus rider twirling on a white horse

"Crack!"

goes the ringmaster's whip.

"Hup! Hup!"

cries the tumbler.

"Bang! Bang! Bang!"

goes the circus rider's heart.

The white horse leaps

into the sandy ring

and the circus rider twirls

in her golden costume.

Stardust and magic,

a night at the circus!

Georges Seurat
The Circus
1891

there is... War in a white dress

Look how
she gallops,
War in a white dress
on a black horse,
with her coal-black hair
streaming in the wind.
How she gallops,
War in her white dress,
laughing and screeching: " Squabble!
at her army of black crows
pecking at the bodies.

Le Douanier Rousseau
War
1894

there are... ugly old men

The first one is grumpy,

The second one is grizzly,

The third one looks like a stuffed cabbage,

The fourth one, like a squashed pear,

and why does the fifth one

look so pleased with himself?

Daumier made them awfully ugly,

uglier than they really were,

to poke fun at them

and make us laugh.

Honoré Daumier
Prunelle
Cunin
Étienne
Fruchard
Comte de Kératry
1832-1833

41

there is... a sleepyhead

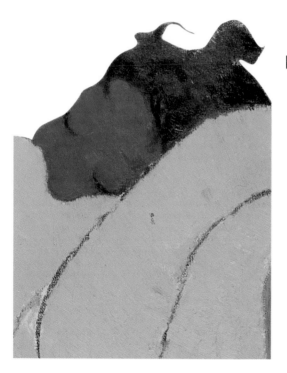

It's morning
but I don't want to get up.
I'm as snug as a bug in a rug
under my cosy blanket
with my head
in soft pillows.
Please let me
stay in bed
a bit longer.
I love sleeping in.

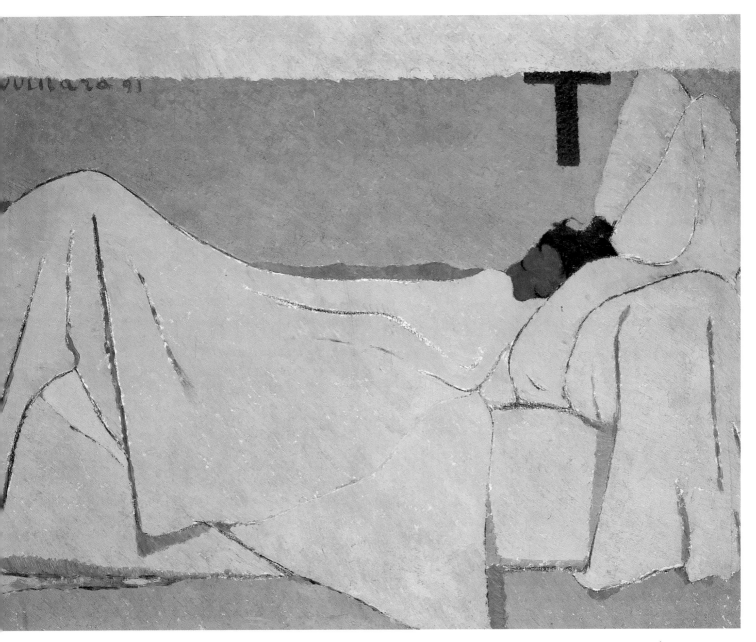

Édouard Vuillard
In Bed
1891

You will find the red dog,

the boy prince, the polar bear

and all the others

at the Orsay Museum.

The museum is open every day,

except Mondays,

and for you, it is free.

Photos:
Réunion des musées nationaux
Photos by D. Arnaudet, G. Blot,
C. Jean, H. Lewandowsky, H. Lagiewski,
A. Morin, R. G. Ojeda.

1st registered: December 2001
Registered: May 2013
ISBN 978-2-7118-4422-7
JC 30 4422